Getting started with
Tambour Embroidery

Saskia ter Welle

Copyright © 2018 Imagos Publishers

Doesburg | The Netherlands

All rights reserved.

Thanks to my dear parents,
who always encouraged me to create.

Thanks to my wonderful husband,
who inspires me to dream and see the world as my playground.

Thanks to God,
who has put in me, as in all of you,
the desire to see, create and enjoy real beauty.

CHAPTER ONE

Introduction

HAUTE COUTURE EMBROIDERY

One of the most eye-catching techniques developed to realize the dreams of haute couture is the art of tambour embroidery. This technique offers a perfect way to work with beads and sequins. These materials reflect the evening lights beautifully and put the wearer of a dress in the spotlights. Charles Frederick Worth (1825-1895), the man we tend to see as the first 'couturier,' was a brilliant man. Why? He created a dressing room for his clients with those typical evening lights, to show them exactly how their dresses would look like during mesmerizing evening dinners. France has since a rich tradition in couture. This tradition is known for its luxurious style, with garments richly adorned with threads, beads, sequins, feathers and other precious materials.

* * *

The world of haute couture is a world of its own. It has its rules and its beauty. The exclusiveness keeps the mystery alive, even when in a time of internet and mass communication information seems so readily available. I am so glad you took the time and effort to purchase this book. It must be because you are curious to know what all the rumor is about. Is tambour embroidery special? Is it difficult? Is it do-able? Yes! Definitely. It is all of that. Like many people in fashion I started to dream about Paris and the glamorous, yet sophisticated evening dresses created by famous fashion houses. What is their secret? How do they adorn their dresses with so much sparkle and refinement?

BOOK EXTRAS

This book is about craftsmanship. It explains in text and photos how to get started with tambour embroidery. Although this will never replace a side-by-side instruction from an expert, it can come pretty close with all the extra materials provided through the links in this book.

Whenever you see a URL like http://etcetera, click on the link, and you will discover the online resources with patterns, more photos and instruction videos. It will be as if you are in my class because I will show you exactly how to mount the embroidery frame, how to handle the tambour hook and how to make the stitch. After reading this book and studying the videos, you know the secret of the tambour hook.

In my book, I direct to my personal website and ETSY webshop as well. I have put years of research and effort in finding quality embroidery materials. They are difficult to find in Paris or on the Internet. For this reason, I have brought them together in my ETSY shop for your convenience.

ECOLE LESAGE

Lesage is one of the most famous embroidery ateliers of Paris. In 1992, Francois Lesage started worrying seeing his older workers die one-by-one. These ladies, who were known for their specialized craftsmanship, would leave this world with all their knowledge. He decided to establish a school where he could pass on the couture embroidery craftsmanship to new generations. In doing so, he started sharing the extraordinary history of Maison Lesage.

I still remember the day that I learned about Ecole Lesage. I almost couldn't believe it. Could this be true? A school where you can learn how to embroider at this level? I immediately added it to my bucket list.

A few years later my husband and children surprised me by giving me a wonderful birthday present: an introduction course in 'Broderie d'Art' at Ecole Lesage in Paris. Having studied French language and culture in my younger years, this would be in many ways a pleasant experience: going to Paris, taking classes there, walking around and breathing this city as if I was living in it.

It was during this first trip to Paris that I got acquainted with cultural differences as well. Being raised in a creative and intellectual family, I experienced an open way of communication on a high level. My high school education had a strong focus on team work as well as on questioning the world around us. I had an independent lifestyle, which did not prepare me for the rigid and bureaucratic structure of Parisian education at that time at Ecole Lesage. What can I say? I was shocked.

Women of somewhere between their twenties and sixties, from all over the world, come to Paris to get educated in embroidery at Ecole Lesage. It is their free choice to come. Some come for fun, others for their professional future. They pay a significant amount of money and travel hours or even days to stay in Paris. Wouldn't this school, where people from all over the world go, be an excellent means to build bridges between countries, nations, and cultures?

It took some willpower for me to return and accept the way of teaching in Paris. The reason that I returned was of course that the embroidery took my heart. I knew I still had a lot to learn. I am happy to see that the atmosphere in the school has changed over the years, and I have a warm connection with the teachers.

* * *

PARIS

The visits to Paris meant to me much more than a nice vacation and a useful learning experience. The traveling, the opportunity to get to know Paris from the inside out and the experience of culture changed my view of what is possible in life.

The schedule for me was like this: I would take classes from 9.30-12.30. At lunch break, I would have a warm meal (typical French, with a glass of wine) to save time in the evening. I would have a look at second-hand books in the galleries and take some more classes from 14-17. In the evening I then had time for a quick run for materials and to continue my work on the assignments for the next day until midnight.

Apart from my schooling at Ecole Lesage, I started going to Paris to search for embroidery materials. What a lovely adventure! Having a purpose while strolling through the streets, it places the city in an entirely different light. I wasn't looking at the touristic highlights, but walking around as an native inhabitant. I did not only search for materials for tambour embroidery but also for couture sewing. In the country where I live, The Netherlands, most fabric stores have closed their doors in the last ten years. Only a few are still open today. A big city like Paris still has so many places to discover!

It didn't take long for me to see that tambour embroidery is exclusive. Not only as a technique, but also in the suppliers of materials. At Ecole Lesage, I only got one name, Fried Frères, where I could buy beads and sequins. That was it. Although this still is one of the most powerful resources in Paris, it does not supply all the other materials, like Fil à Gant, chenille or raffia.

***

FRIED FRÈRES

Fried Frères, a company based in Paris and established in 1886 by Gustave Fried, has a rich history of trading glass beads, buttons, cabochons, rhinestones, Parisian fashion novelties and accessories, hats, gloves and Bohemian crystal glass, thus making the connection with the heart of couture business. Fried Frères has their roots in the Jablonec region of the Czech Republic. Joblonec is the place to go for beads and glass components.

Looking for all the other supplies that I needed for broderie d'art, I started searching the internet for additional suppliers. The city of Lunéville as a historical place of craftsmanship for the tambour hook, also called the Lunéville hook. I ordered some materials at the local embroidery museum of Lunéville.

LUNÉVILLE

Lunéville, a city in the eastern part of France, has a history of embroidery with the tambour hook. From about 1810 many women worked on cotton tulle using the tambour hook and formed lace with the chain stitch. Later the same technique was used to apply beads and sequins. In the castle of Lunéville, you find a museum, shop and school around this craft. The family managing the facility is eager to preserve this heritage for future generations.

My husband has his private pilot license, and we travel through Europe for business. During one of our trips, we decided to visit the city of Lunéville to see what this town is like and what the museum shop has to offer. I had started to think about my future, and I knew that I needed more resources for materials than Fried Frères in Paris alone.

I called the people at the museum and asked if it would be possible to interview someone of the museum or embroidery school for my blog about embroidery? And if they could tell us the nearest aerodrome to land? Although they were not sure if an interview was possible, we made an arrangement that we would come over during our flying trip. At the moment of landing, we discovered that the whole village had come to look at the plane. It wasn't that common that someone from abroad would land there! Taking a taxi to the Chateau, the location of the embroidery museum, we wondered what happened to this lovely region of France. The whole area looked desolated and poor. Not a place where you imagine the creation of beauty.

The castle looked great even though there had recently been a fire in part of the building. It had been build by the same architect as the Chateau de Versailles, and it looked vibrant and romantic. I still remember the excitement I felt, standing in front of this castle, stating in front of a camera that I was about to enter the museum for tambour embroidery. The cold shower I experienced ten minutes later was a big surprise.

Entering the shop of the museum, the lady started to talk to me in French in front of all French people, telling me all the bad things of The Netherlands and Dutch people in general, not knowing me at all. I already was a client of hers, ordered several times through the internet and came to show my interest in what they were doing. I was supposed to take the blame for all my countries faults (like drinking coffee milk in our coffee (shame!), all (is that right? I didn't know) people using drugs. Interesting. My husband soon decided to go and sit outside in the sun, and not interfere. I wondered 'What do I do now?' I came all the way to see the museum, do an interview if possible (which was out of the question now) and buy my much-needed supplies. The only thing left for me was: ignoring the lady, selecting the supplies I needed and leave as soon as possible. And so I did exactly that.

Thinking about giving embroidery classes in The Netherlands, I was wondering how I could start without the proper materials. That was a problem I still had to solve. I also had to find an answer to the question: where do my future students buy their beads and sequins if they don't know the French language?

BACK TO PARIS

The beauty of Ecole Lesage, when I started, was the close connection between the school and the ateliers located in the same building. People attending the ateliers would ring the bell and walk through the school. Fabrics would pile up in the hallway. Those small details added to a nice 'ambiance.' Recently, the ateliers have been moved to Pantin, one of the outskirts of Paris.

The center of Paris wasn't just inspiring by its buildings and people; it also was an amazing place by offering all the specialized stores you can think of, like for example Librairie Passage Jouffroy, where you can buy the most excellent books about art, fashion and embroidery.

FAVORITE ADDRESSES

Curious about my favorite addresses in Paris? Have a look at this web page: http://tinyurl.com/jctsr8o.

Having lunch like the French for me was key in the days I was in Paris to take classes: eating a warm lunch while enjoying a nice glass of wine or a pot of green tea just brings you in a good mood.

In spite of the wonderful experiences I had had, I soon started wondering what would happen if I would take my new acquired knowledge of embroidery to The Netherlands and start teaching classes there. What would I do differently? What would I do the same?

I decided to take a chance and do it my way. Integrating my passion for fashion and couture with the love for coffee and hospitality, I wanted to create a whole experience in one place, where people can come to learn new techniques, be welcomed with coffee and tea and a nice lunch and where they have lots of possibilities to connect with other individuals with the same interest. Integrating craftsmanship with business knowledge, the use of internet and defining one's niche market: all coming together in the specialized training course 'Mastering Broderie d'Art'.

As I write this book, women find their way in the field of couture embroidery after having finished my courses. Many of my students recognized their inner need for creating beauty and finding out their personal strengths. It is when you bring your talent to the world, that you start living the life meant for you. To discover this for yourself takes time and effort, but I have seen the transformation in the life of both myself and my students. It pays off in many ways.

In this book, you find the basis of what is happening in my

atelier. It shows the first steps in haute couture embroidery by using the tambour hook. Will it be your start for a new, adventurous journey?

Have a close look. And don't forget to enjoy every step along the way.

Warm greetings,

Saskia ter Welle

Remember: don't believe a word of what I say. Test everything and save what you like. I can only speak from my experience and so you might very well have a different opinion or a different experience. Please share your knowledge with the world. Together we know more.

CHAPTER TWO
Tambour Embroidery Explained

THE TAMBOUR HOOK

While some people know how to handle a needle and thread, and others are familiar with the existence of a tambour needle, the number of people knowing how to manage and use the tambour needle are rare. And that is a pity because the possibilities of this beautiful tool are sheer endless.

In this book, I will show you the beauty of tambour embroidery. For many years, the tambour needle was only used to embroider chain stitches on fabric like cotton tulle or linen with threads in different colors. When done well, it gives you excellent and even results.

However, when a smart man discovered a way to apply beads and sequins with that same technique of making a chain stitch, it changed the fashion world dramatically. Using beads and sequins became an entirely different art.

* * *

In this book you will not find an extensive study on the history of tambour embroidery, nor will you find everything there is to know. I will give you the information that is needed to make a start in tambour embroidery yourself.

WHAT IS TAMBOUR EMBROIDERY?

Tambour embroidery is a form of embroidery with the use of a particular tool: the tambour hook on a tambour frame. The hook is a gaunt crochet hook with a sharp point. By making stitches through fabric with thread, a pattern forms on the material. With one basic stitch you can easily draw lines and fill patterns simply by using different threads in various thicknesses and colors. This basic stitch is called the chain stitch ('point de chaînette' in French). Another way to use the tambour hook is to apply beads and sequins. You work beads and sequins with the same basic chain stitch in between the beads or sequins on your thread. Later in this book I will explain this technique in detail.

* * *

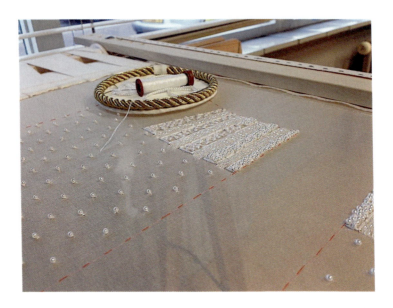

The term 'tambour' refers to the fabric you work on, mounted on a frame in a way that it looks like a 'tambour' (the French word for 'drum'). When you work on this frame, you need both hands to handle the hook, the thread and eventually the beads and sequins. You place the embroidery frame on a set of trestles to keep both hands free for the actual embroidery.

Many people get confused by all the different terms that are used in embroidery. In this book, I use the term tambour embroidery referring to the use of the tambour hook. Forget all the confusion about names. People use the same word for different techniques. The embroidery itself is what matters. Not the words to describe it. They may help, but are not the essence of the beauty of what you can create.

* * *

BRODERIE D'ART

The technique of the tambour hook is part of 'Broderie d'Art', a French term which refers to an endless range of embroidery techniques used for haute couture. The essence of Broderie d'Art is creating a fairy tale in fabric. Using all sorts of materials together in a three-dimensional embroidery design, which is reflecting the light in different ways, draws the attention. Your eyes search for the details. Wonderful.

The tambour hook provides a way to do a lot of the embroidery faster. At least, when you have mastered the technique. Don't expect this to happen overnight. It requires quite some effort to get a grasp of it and then, even more time to do it fast.

Please do not confuse the term tambour embroidery with 'bead work'. Bead work is the art or craft of attaching beads to one another by stringing them with a needle and thread or wire, or sewing them to cloth, not necessarily using the tambour hook. Bead work can be used in couture as well as in jewelry.

My fascination for tambour embroidery lies in the connection to French haute couture and the combination of this technique with other techniques to create a complete, diverse, three-dimensional decoration to quality garments.

Time and again artists from around the world are happy to add tambour embroidery to their art as well. They use it in different ways: adding glamor to photography using shiny materials, or adding structure to textile projects or paintings.

CHAPTER THREE
Basic Tools and Materials

TOOLS

When you start with tambour embroidery, you need specific tools. There is an important function behind all these tools. Some tools you may replace by using something else that is more or less similar that you already have. Others are just essential to buy.

What I consider as essential are the following: a large embroidery frame, rectangular, two pieces of each five meters of cotton twill tape of 3 cm wide, a tambour hook, a bobbin holder and silk organza.

PRACTICAL

There are some practical items you may like to purchase as well: two trestles, Fil à Gant, threaded beads, threaded sequins and an erasable pencil. Some added notions to make your embroidery more exciting could be embroidery threads, cotton sewing thread, beading needles, pins, small embroidery scissors with a sharp point, a small jewelry plier and Swarovski stones.

QUALITY

If there is one thing I know for sure that works for me, that would be choosing quality over quantity. Choose the best quality you can afford for the tools with which you work. Compare it to any craftsmanship: using the right tools makes all the difference. I recommend you to start investing in the best tools you can find. It adds to the joy of learning.

It took me years to find the right tools for my students. In the end, I developed some of them myself.

WHERE TO BUY

My preferred choice of materials is available at: https://www.etsy.com/shop/saskiaterwelle.

EMBROIDERY FRAME

You place your fabric in a frame in order to obtain the right tension in the fabric. Choosing the right embroidery frame is key. Allow me to explain to you why. The material you use is fragile. However, you have to put a strain on it. The only way you can do this is by dividing the tension well.

In a standard embroidery hoop, the material will loosen easily. A hoop also prevents you from working with both hands. When you would work with an embroidery hoop in a holder, you can collaborate with both hands, but you won't be able to work efficiently on both sides of the fabric. With tambour embroidery, you work on both sides of the fabric: the right side and the wrong side. You will want to use a frame that can be turned quickly every five minutes.

It is wise to use a loose, rectangular frame when you are serious about learning this technique. Make sure the frame you choose is suitable for your purpose. Is the wood finished smoothly? Will the color of the twill tape not dispense to your work? The frame needs to be sturdy and smooth and the knobs easy to use.

I recommend starting to work on an individual frame with a length of about one meter. That size is not too big in most rooms, and you can quite easily take it with you. It is the ideal size for making decorations for hats, to embroider bags or even make an embroidered corset. For larger projects, like big embroidered paintings, embroidered dresses or bridal gowns, you might need a bigger atelier frame.

***

Many people ask me if you can make a frame yourself. Sure! But keep my recommendations in mind. You can find a description of the frame here: http://tinyurl.com/zhyusto.

TWILL TAPE

When you have the right embroidery frame, you will see it has twill tape on both long sides attached to the frame. This cotton tape is quite thick, for it to be durable enough to use every time you mount your frame.

Besides this strong twill tape, you also need a pair of softer, cotton twill tape to put tension on the fabric on the short side of the frame. In the next chapter, I will explain how this works in detail. For now, you need to know that this tape should be 3 cm wide and 5 meters long, and preferably come in a light color.

You never cut these tapes. Using it for every project, you might not always need the whole length of it. When you do not need the full range, you just leave it and pin it to the rest of the tape until required for a next project.

THREADED BEADS AND SEQUINS

The beauty of working beads and sequins with the tambour hook is that it goes fast. Even more so, by using beads and sequins that are pre-strung to a thread. You might think: 'I have a lot of loose beads in stock of a previous project, let's use them for tambour embroidery.

***

Of course you might do so, but consider these two facts as well: first, embroidery beads are usually smaller than what you buy for making jewelry or other crafts projects. Using these bigger beads give a less refined image to your work. And second, it takes time to thread your beads. The time you just want to gain by using the tambour hook. Buying beads on a string saves you a lot of time.

TAMBOUR HOOK OR NEEDLE

The pinnacle of ingenuity: the tambour hook forms the basis of tambour embroidery. This embroidery hook is a superfine crochet needle in a holder. Often the holder is made of wood, but you can find beautiful examples of this tool in silver or other precious materials as well. A screw holds the needle in place. Make sure that every time you use the needle, the hook is on the same side as the pin. If not, verify that the pin is loose, then turn it in the right direction, and fasten the screw.

* * *

The tip of the needle is extremely sharp. I advise you, when not using the needle, to prick the needle in a piece of cork. You protect the material from accidental damage and prevent injury to yourselves or others. The holder has to be one without wooden splinters for the same reason not to hurt yourselves or damage the material.

STANDARD SIZE OF NEEDLE

The most common size used for haute couture embroidery is needle size 80. When you use thicker threads, you might want to choose a bigger needle. Needles are available from size 70 up to 110. Some holders are appropriate for only one size. Always check if you can just change the needle, or need a handle with every needle.

* * *

SILK ORGANZA

Although you may apply tambour embroidery to almost any fabric, I strongly recommend you to start learning this skill by using silk organza. This fabric is both stable and transparent (especially the lighter colors), which makes it possible to see what both your hands are doing, both under and over the frame.

Forget cheap polyester organza: it will rip apart and look awful! Not worth the effort in embroidery.

TRESTLES

For a nice working height, you put two trestles under your frame. You might use the back of two chairs; a chair and a table top, or any other construction you can create that works for you. The main issue is that you need your frame to have a good working height, still being able to turn the frame around quickly when needed (quite often).

In most local DIY stores you may find simple trestles. These are quite cheap and foldable, so very convenient when you do not have a lot of room. When your work a lot behind your frame, you will be happy with trestles that you can adjust in height. I bought mine at the famous Swedish warehouse, and I am quite happy with them. They also look beautiful in the living room at home. By putting the frame on two trestles with different heights up front and in the back, you can choose to even work at an angle.

FIL À GANT

Fil à Gant is a thread with a special finish, which makes it both strong and smooth. This finish makes the thread strong enough to hold glass beads solidly in place, without getting in trouble with your thread tying down. Although this is the easiest thread to start with, you can use standard sewing thread as well.

BOBBIN HOLDER

A bobbin holder is a simple wooden piece of equipment, formed by a pin and a round plate. You put the small part of the pin in a hole in your frame or trestle. The large pin is used to place your bobbin on, resting on the round plate. The bobbin holder needs to be long enough to hold your bobbin well, while small enough to be put in a hole of your frame or trestle.

* * *

Although it is quite a simple piece of wood, the importance for the embroiderer is great, while it prevents your spool with thread from rolling through the whole room. To me this tool, which keeps me from getting insane, is magic!

BEADING NEEDLE

Sometimes you need to 'fix' a bead or sequin, or you want to add a bead somewhere without the tambour hook. For this purpose, you need a 'beading needle', which comes in several sizes, both lengthwise as thickness-wise.

The beading needle is fragile, and it passes through the eye of most small beads. Threading this needle is hard, especially when you get older. Don't hesitate to use glasses or a loupe.

* * *

BEAD SPINNER

A 'bead spinner' is a super smart tool. By turning the bead spinner around, the loose beads just pile up on the needle you put in the turning container: amazing! The usual needle for the bead spinner is too thick for embroidery beads, so make sure to have a beading needle in the right size at hand. With some practice, it works well, despite the fact that the beading needle won't have the same curve as the one provided with the 'bead spinner' when you buy one.

LOUPE FOR GLASSES

Many people wear glasses. In addition to their glasses, a loupe for glasses is the perfect tool to see even the smallest stitches made with the tambour hook. The loupe moves with your head and does not get in the way while embroidering. A separate loupe, one that you put above your work of embroidery, is most of the time just hindering you. Order one with your local optician. A well-known brand for these loupes is Eschenbach.

ERASABLE FABRIC PENCIL

To mark your pattern on the fabric, you may use a regular pencil. This accessible tool works well on many materials, so you won't have a problem to start with this. But, when you are working on delicate fabrics for expensive projects, an erasable fabric pencil will be worth the purchase. You can quickly erase the lines drawn with this pen without leaving a trace. Just use a piece of gum or a wet cloth. It is available in different colors to be visible on every type of fabric.

CHAPTER FOUR

Mounting the Frame

USING AN EMBROIDERY FRAME

Holding a piece of cloth in your hands while embroidering, will make the fabric pull together, even if you take care and treat your thread with delicacy. As a result, often the lines will 'wither' and 'wobble' once you have finished the embroidery. By working on a frame, you solve this problem. You stretch the fabric and work on an even background. For any embroidery, this is the way to go.

HOW TO MOUNT THE FRAME

Mounting a frame is not too difficult. However, it can be a little annoying because you need to do it precisely. If not done precisely, you are going to regret that later on in the process. The reason is, that you if you screw up, you have to repeat the whole tedious 'mounting the frame' process again. So please, take notice of the step-by-step approach and proceed carefully.

***

You may want to see a video on this topic. Please go to: http://tinyurl.com/j5evlbe.

You can change the subtitling to English if it is not correctly shown the first time you watch.

Like with any crafts project, tambour embroidery is just the same. The foundation is in good and accurate preparation. The first times you mount a frame, it might make you feel clumsy. Making straight stitches at specific lengths, holding twill tape and fabric together under tension: all this handling is different from what you are used to do. Be sure to know that this will get better after having done this a few times. So let's start.

ON THE LONG SIDE OF THE FRAME

Take a rectangular piece of silk organza of about 40 to 60 centimeters. Rip this fabric to make sure every side is perfectly straight. Remove the selvedge or selvage of the fabric (the 'stiff' side of the fabric, sometimes shown by a different weave), because this might change the tension of the material when mounted in the frame. Iron the fabric. Pin the long side of your fabric to the long side of the frame (in the middle) with five pins, keeping the edge of the fabric just even with the edge of the tape, thus making sure that everything will be pulled straight when putting tension on the frame. Sew the fabric onto the twill tape on the frame with a double thread of strong (iron) sewing thread. Make sure your stitches are no longer than 1 cm. Start and finish your thread by making three stitches at the same place over the edge of your fabric.

***

Do the same at the other long side of the frame with the other edge of the fabric. Make sure the fabric will be of the same length as the first side by putting the long sides of the frame next to each other and matching sides. By working carefully now, you will prevent later damage on the fabric.

It is time to put the frame together. Put the short sides of the frame on the ends of the long sides and fix the knobs. Insert the screws on the short sides and put the round metal plate and knob on the long sides.

Do you feel the tension on the fabric? Fantastic. You are beginning to form your 'tambour', the absolute basis for tambour embroidery.

The next step will be attaching the twill tape of 3 cm width from the edges of the fabric around the short sides of the frame.

ON THE SHORT SIDE

Make sure the long and short sides of the frame are at a right angle from each other, forming a perfect rectangular. Take one of the 5-meter twill tapes of 3 cm width (rolled up) and pin one end to the side part of the fabric, 2 centimeters from the side; pin every pin twice in-and-out. Wrap the twill tape over and under the sidebar of the frame, pinning it again to the fabric at a distance of 2 cm from the side, twice with the same pin. Now wrap the twill tape under-over and pin it to the fabric. Repeat this process unto the end of the fabric. Pin the remaining twill tape under the tape in place for later use (do not cut it off). Repeat this process for the other side of the fabric. You will see 'V' shapes appearing when done the right way.

* * *

Use a little strength for the first side, a lot for the second side to get the right tension on the fabric.

The tension of the material differs from day to day, caused by changes in the temperature and humidity in the room. Always check if the pressure is still right. If not, just unscrew one knob and put a little tension back by extending the frame.

Now you are ready to put your frame on the trestles.

CHAPTER FIVE
The Chain Stitch

SOME COMMENTS FIRST

With tambour embroidery, you work with the thread on the bobbin. You only cut the thread after you are have finished the stitching. You place your bobbin always on the bobbin holder: on the left when you are right handed, on the right when you are left handed.

Decide to work when possible with one hand on top of the frame, and one hand under the frame. It takes some time to practice this and getting used to, but eventually it saves you an enormous amount of time. The real deal: starting to develop a proper eye-hand coördination.

Always first pull the thread through the fabric and keep it in place with the hand with which you hold the tambour needle (probably right), and squeeze the thread between the palm of your hand and your fingers. Make a tiny little stitch forward and then back again and pull on the thread: this is your beginning stitch (when it has formed a small knot on top of the fabric).

THE STITCH

Put the small knob of the needle in the direction where you are aiming. Hold the hook like a pen, close to the button. Prick the needle vertically through the fabric. Wrap the thread around the needle and turn the needle half way around (180 degrees). Make sure you only move to the 'open side' of your hand and not 'under' your hand. Place your needle at a 45-degree angle and put a little strain on the fabric with the needle, while pulling the needle up. By doing so, you create a hole between the threads of the fabric, thus making room for the hook of your needle. Immediately turn the needle back in the direction you are going to, making sure you keep the thread on the hook of the needle. Put the needle vertically in the fabric for the next stitch.

If you feel resistance while pulling your thread upwards, you might need to make more room for the hook by putting a strain on the fabric with the needle. Another reason for resistance can be that you tend to keep the tension on the thread under too tight, thus making it impossible for the needle to move.

* * *

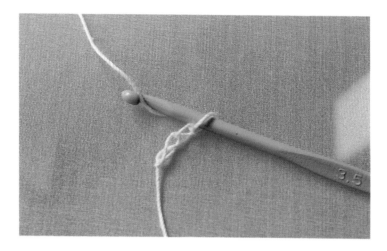

Now check your stitch. Does it look like two lines straight next to each other? Or do you see a twist in the loop? In that case, you can adopt the way you turn your needle. At the end of your line of stitches, you finish your chain by stitching three times in the same hole in the fabric. This way the thread forms three small knots on top of each other. When you have done this, you can cut off the thread. Working on the right side of the fabric, you bring the end of the thread to the wrong side with the tambour hook (holding it under the frame).

Register on my website to get exclusive access to the secrets of tambour embroidery. Two main techniques will be demonstrated to you. One is the chain stitch and the other technique is transferring beads and sequins. Registration is exclusive to readers of my book and of course for free. Don't skip this step. It might be crucial for you in understanding the rest of this book.

Here is the link: http://tinyurl.com/gvouvwf.

MY PHILOSOPHY

How do you get to master this technique? Some of you are perfectionists. You are the people that tend to redo everything that is not perfect right at the beginning. Others are easy and do not have a serious look at how their stitching is performing and are happy with bad results.

In my opinion, you need a little bit of both approaches. You need a 'laisser faire' attitude to get into the right 'flow' or 'rhythm', but you also need to look close and decide on what looks good and what needs repair.

Find the right mixture of both to get ahead. Enjoy the process. And soon you will discover how this incredible technique of tambour embroidery can transform your life.

* * *

FINAL COMMENTS

Cut off all your beginning- and finishing threads immediately. The dangling threads may inadvertently be 'embroidered' along at the back of your work, leaving you with a messy result. For me, it works best if the embroidery looks as beautiful at the back as at the front.

Exercise: draw some original lines on your fabric and start practicing the chain stitch in all directions. In the beginning, you will experience difficulty changing direction. It is hard to do the whole stitching procedure first in one way, and then, by turning around, do it the other way as well. By starting in straight lines and working to circles, you soon will learn how to handle this.

CHAPTER SIX
Applying Beads

BEADS

The great magical moment is when you get to know how to apply beads with the tambour hook. It is the time when everything falls into place, and you discover the trick. Be prepared for some real excitement!

When you apply beads with needle and thread, you cut the thread and make a knot. Then you take one bead at a time and sew it to the fabric by going through the hole of the bead with a thin beading needle, and pulling the thread through the bead. That's it.

Applying beads with the tambour hook works quite differently. You take your bobbin with the thread, preferably Fil à Gant, and bring the beads from the thread to the thread on the bobbin. I will explain this a little later. Now you can start making chain stitches in between the beads. So you don't work through the beads, but you take the thread and pull it up between the beads, thus making sure they stay perfectly in place.

TRANSFERRING

So you bought some beautiful embroidery beads on a string. Time to transfer them to the Fil à Gant on your bobbin. There are two ways to do so. The first one is by knotting the thread of the beads to the Fil à Gant and carefully transfer them over the knot to the other side. The second one is by pricking with your tambour hook through the thread of the beads and pull the Fil à Gant through the thread (without a knot) and carefully transfer the beads to the other side. The first option is the easiest, but the second alternative works, even with very tiny holes in the beads, as well. Watch the process on video here: http://tinyurl.com/gvouvwf.

Now you have transferred the beads to the embroidery thread you can start with the beginning stitch as you did before. Be careful that the beads can fall to the ground as long as the beginning stitch has not been secured well.

First, you prick the needle vertically through the fabric. Then you place one bead straight to the fabric, and you keep it in place with the forefinger of your left hand. Take the thread with the needle while it lies just on top of the inner side of your forefinger and bring it up in one, flowing movement. It is the same movement as with the chain stitch, but you put a bead in between. It is crocheting through the fabric.

* * *

It helps to talk out loud all the steps until you know them by heart. Although this seems unnatural, most people need a few days to get this right. No worries. Just practice and enjoy. Put on classical music, concentrate and see how the pattern appears on the fabric. Isn't this beautiful?

STITCH LENGTH

Beads come in different forms, shapes, finishes and sizes. For haute couture embroidery, the most common sizes are 13/0 and 15/0. These are delicate beads that create the subtleness we are looking for in excellent artwork.

Besides round shaped beads there are 3-cuts (beautiful shine in the spotlights!) and 2-cut beads. The last ones can be long as well and are called 'tubes' (French) or bugle beads.

What influence does the size of a bead have on the length of your stitch? Or does it work the other way around: is the size of the stitch of any influence on the bead?

Definitely! A proper stitch length is the size of the bead plus a little extra. That 'little extra' depends on the form of the design and the 'room' the bead needs in that line. For example: if you stitch beads in a circle, there is more space for the bead than in a straight line. Therefore, in a circle, the stitch length can be smaller than in a straight line.

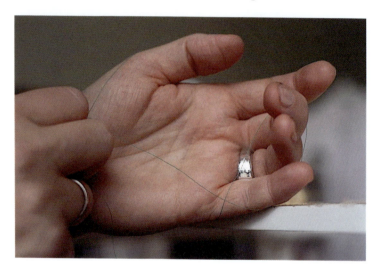

How to keep the thread.

When using bugle beads, the stitch length should be quite long, but the same rule applies.

The only way to make sure that you use the correct stitch length is by checking it. Even the most experienced embroiderers check themselves.

How? By stitching a few centimeters and then turning the

frame to see how it looks. Just that. Simple but a very effective method.

CHAPTER SEVEN
Applying Sequins

FORMS AND SHAPES

Sequins come in different forms, finishes, shapes and sizes. For haute couture embroidery, the flat sequins of 4 mm are most common. Sizes differ from 2 mm to 7 mm with a hole in the middle. Bigger sequins usually have a hole on one side and are not pre-strung.

Applying sequins does not differ too much from using beads. The only difference is the length of the stitch: for sequins, the length is a little smaller than half the size of the sequin. This way the hole in the middle of the sequin will be covered by the next one, giving a smooth and neat line of sequins 'en rivière' (like a river).

Selecting one sequin at a time is the only difficulty. I'm always happy if the nail of my left thumb is quite long: it helps me in selecting the sequins by rubbing between my fingers and flipping a sequin with my nail.

***

Before you transfer the sequins from the thread to the Fil à Gant, decide what is the right side of the sequin. The right side is smooth, with rounded corners. The wrong side looks 'cut off'. Sometimes you can discover the right side by watching the finish of the sequin. Either way: you loosen the knot on the right side and bring the sequins over to your bobbin. This way the right side will be up when you have embroidered the sequin.

APPLYING SEQUINS

So you transferred your sequins. Make a beginning stitch. Move some sequins to the fabric with your left hand, all the way up to the fabric. Wrap the thread around your left hand, keeping your thumb and forefinger free. Make sure that the sequins stay close to the cloth. Pick the sequins one by one with your thumb and pointer. Keep the sequin in place with the forefinger of your left hand. Prick the tambour hook vertically through the fabric. Select one sequin with your dumb and forefinger. Pick up the thread with the tambour hook and pull it up the same way as you did before (at an angle of 45 degrees in the direction you are going to, while putting a strain on the needle; making a 'hole' in the fabric for the hook of the tambour needle). This same procedure works for cup sequins.

***

There is one important issue I want to share with you about sequins 'in a river'. As I already explained, sequins in a river give a smooth line. Beautiful. Imagine following this line with your finger. How will you do so? You will 'go with the flow' and follow the sequins in a way that does not interrupt the flow. So you start with your finger at the sequin on top and go from there back.

What consequences does this have to the start and finish of your line? Exactly! You start at proposed ending of the line, going back to where you would follow the line with your finger. Don't forget this. It changes the aspect of your embroidery. It makes all the difference. In an embroidery pattern you would want to add this information. The appropriate way to do so, is by adding an arrow at the start of the embroidery in the right direction.

See some examples of first time projects on this page: http://tinyurl.com/zsjs6gw.

CHAPTER EIGHT
Large Frames

THE CHALLENGE

For seasoned embroiderers who are not familiar with an embroidery frame, tambour embroidery is a challenge. Even if you do embroidery with needle and thread, working with the frame is different because you now keep the left hand under and the right hand over the frame. You need even in that case to find a way for both hands to work together. Add to this the additional complexity of the tambour hook and you challenge is complete.

In this chapter, we will discuss a few additional techniques. Only using beads can be quite boring. You make your embroidery more attractive with a combination of different materials.

TRANSFERRING THE PATTERN

Depending on the size of the project, there are several ways to transfer your pattern to the fabric. I will explain to you three examples. First of all, put your pattern under the organza fabric with one hand and draw the lines with a pencil with your other hand. The second option would be to put your design under the organza fabric, pin it in place with some pins, and draw the lines with an erasable pencil. Finally you could take your pattern and use your sewing machine to prick holes along the lines by following those lines with the needle without using sewing thread; just making holes. Place the pattern on top of the fabric and rub some chalk or other colored powder over the pattern. The pattern will show on the fabric. Use some stabiliser (hair spray?) to prevent the lines from disappearing.

WORKING WITH EMBROIDERY THREAD

When you are filling larger surfaces with embroidery, choosing embroidery yarn is more pleasing to the eye. Even more so, if you use it in contrast with beads and sequins. The flat surface and just that little shine make the other more reflecting materials stand out. Silkshading makes the perfect match with tambour embroidery.

The usual embroidery yarn can be divided or split into thin threads (6-8). Using them as one large thread gives a bold expression; using just some of these threads leads to refinement and gives a more refined effect.

This yarn made of cotton is, of course, a beautiful, natural product. However, I prefer to work with silks. Why? Because silk has a natural shine to it, that is incomparable to cotton, which is matte.

STARTING AND FINISHING YOUR THREAD

Starting and finishing your embroidery thread can be done in different ways. I prefer to do it as follows. Take a double yarn, just cut a long thread, put it on the needle and pull it through until it is folded. Work on the right side of the fabric.

Prick your needle in the middle of the surface you want to cover, for example in the midst of a leaf or circle you would like to fill. Put the end of the thread down on the fabric and stitch it in place with three little stitches. Start filling the surface with the flat stitch. You will cover the beginning stitches with your embroidery. When you finish the thread, again make three small stitches in between the previous ones. They will disappear under the existing embroidery. When you work this way, the back of the embroidery will look almost as beautiful as the front.

ON TOP

Your embroidery improves and gets more intense and intriguing by using beads, sequins or other materials like Swarovski stones on top of your almost finished work. Make your personal statement and put emphasis on what you have created. These details make your design more sophisticated.

DETAILS

Making the details right just before finishing your work is very satisfying to do. It is the 'finishing touch'. Work on the right side of the fabric where you can see the impact of what you are doing.

First, place some materials of your choice in different ways, and see how it looks like. Does it add to the expression of the embroidery? Does it put the focus where it needs to be? You could make pictures of different ways to do it, so you can refer to this later and compare the options. If you are not happy yet, try to place it differently. Take some distance and see how the total picture looks like while closing your eyes half-way. When you are satisfied with the result, apply the materials with care.

Use cotton thread. Cut twice the length of your underarm. Longer threads get twined. Use the thread double. This prevents you from losing it while working, so you still have one arm-length. Start with a small knot on the wrong side of your embroidery, or stitch your thread down like you did with the embroidery thread. Use what works best in your situation. Apply beads in the same direction as the stitches of embroidery. One stitch can handle two or three beads at the same time. When making a longer row, go one bead back, take that bead again on your needle and add one or two more, repeating this process to the end of your line. Apply sequins in a row or with a bead on top to finish it nicely while going back only through the sequin and not through the bead. Use Swarovski 'roses montées' by putting the stones into place and stitching it to the fabric from all four sides to the middle hole and finishing the thread well.

COMPLETING THE EMBROIDERY

You have already discovered the beauty of the chainstitch. I have to tell you the downside: a chainstitch is fragile. Once a stitch is broken, the whole line of stitches tends to get ripped off. How do you make sure your stitches stay in place? Is there a way to solve this problem? First of all, use strong enough thread to hold the material. When using glass beads, a row of beads can weigh a lot. Normal sewing thread will not always do the job. Fil à Gant will. Second, make sure you start and finish with a strong beginning and stopping stitch.

And last, finish the back of your embroidery with a very soft touch of glue. This can be done by putting some Fray check on top of your fingers, then to just rub lightly on the back of the fabric. Alternatively, use some liquid Arabic gum. Another option for embroidery protection that covers the whole piece of fabric is to put a layer of Vliesofix at the back side.

CHAPTER NINE
Good to Know

INSTRUCTIONS FOR CARE

If you would ask me, I wouldn't take a chance and wash or dry clean any clothing with beads and sequins on it. The danger of damaging the work is just too big. In theaters, clothes are cleaned with a cloth with alcohol on the armpit section. That is all you would want to do.

When you want to add an alternative patch on for example a jacket, you would make it as an application. You sew the embroidery on the jacket and remove it before dry cleaning. After the cleaning you sew it on by hand again.

MAKING AN APPLICATION

For applications, it is best to cover the fabric completely with your embroidery. It gives a nice finish if you have beads on the side corners. To complete your embroidery for an application, please follow these instructions.

***

Keep an iron under the frame while the fabric is still in the frame. Then wrap a wet cloth around the iron. Steam will form because of the wet cloth. It will be just enough steam to make the fibers of the silk organza return to its original shape after being stretched by the tambour hook. The small gaps in the fabric will disappear. Do not touch the fabric with your iron. Just keep it close. Otherwise you might damage the sequins in your embroidery from too much heat. Or you might melt plastic parts away. Be very cautious.

Turn the frame, so the back of the fabric is up. Cut a piece of Vliesofix or Bondaweb. The piece just needs to be a little bigger than your embroidery. Place the Vliesofix/Bondaweb on the wrong side of the fabric under your embroidery and iron it softly in place with the paper side up. Cut the embroidery with a seam of 0,5 cm out of the frame. Remove the paper of the Vliesofix/Bondaweb. Make small cuts to the embroidery and fold the seam of the Vliesofix/Bondaweb to the wrong side of the embroidery. Your application is now ready.

SEQUINNED AND EMBROIDERED FABRICS

You might wonder why do all the work yourselves while you can buy beautifully embroidered fabric by the meter? What is the difference?

The main issue is that these fabrics are not exclusive. You will not be the only one using this textile. Second, to use these materials, you have to cut and repair along the seams, which takes a lot of time. Third, you can never make it personal for the person wearing the garment, which you can with a design made by you.

* * *

If you need some quick glamor, then of course these fabrics are a beautiful way to add sparkle to a party dress. It takes a lot of time to master the tambour hook to make it your own. It just depends on your level of quality and what you envision to do. Both is fine.

BEAD SPINNER

Whoever works with beads has undoubtedly had to deal with this: all the beads falling on the floor or the table or the embroidery frame. Usually, I wipe the beads (sorted by color) together and put them in a jar. But sometimes there are too many of the same type, and I would like to look for a different solution.

So when I started to see if there are other options, I stumbled upon the following, that I am happy to share with you now. Take a vacuum cleaner and put a pantyhose around the tip. Vacuum clean the beads. As you'll see, the beads will assemble in the pantyhose. You can now collect them in a cup or any other storage bin to keep them safe.

Although time-consuming and tedious, you may want to save your precious beads by stringing them, especially when they are needed to finish your project properly.

* * *

For this task, a bead spinner is a perfect solution. I bought one through ETSY, but if you Google it or look for it on Pinterest, you may even find ways to make one yourself. I enjoy my version of wood, which adds to the character of craftsmanship in the atelier. Be sure to have some real thin beading needles at hand, because the bead spinner usually is used for collecting the bigger beads used for making jewelry, and the according needles provided with the spinner will not work well with embroidery beads.

STORAGE AND TRANSPORT

It is one thing to make a beautiful embroidery and assemble all the necessary tools. What to do when you want to store and transport them? Because of the nature of your tools – scissors and needles – you want to make sure nobody can get hurt and nothing will get damaged along the way. So you need something strong to protect. What I show my students, is the little box I use, that I got with a new pair of sunglasses.

Just the right size and material! I use it already for years.

SILK, COTTON AND MORE

For sewing and embroidery alike, I love to work with yarns with a natural origin. I prefer to use silk splitting thread because it gives such a refined, soft shine. For the various smaller tasks during the embroidery process, such as applying loose beads and Swarovski stones, I like to use cotton thread. Sewing thread usually is made of polyester. You may use this as well.

Fil à Gant, the preferred yarn for applying beads and sequins with the tambour hook, is made of cotton. This thread is mercerized, which means that the yarn has been processed with alkaline solutions to be smoother, shinier and stronger.

Widely used are metalized yarns. They are among my favorites. Metallic yarn usually has a core thread, wrapped with a metallic thread. When this wrapping thread quickly strips up, it can create a severe delay while embroidering. You need to finish your thread and start again when this happens. Always look for metallic yarn that is as smooth as possible. I am utterly charmed by the threads of Fil au Chinois.

WHICH FABRICS ARE SUITABLE?

People often ask me: 'What fabrics are suitable for tambour embroidery'? The quick answer is almost any fabric.

A harder to handle fabric is jersey or tricot, which is a knitted fabric with stretch. As a result, it is hard to put tension on the fabric in a frame. Therefore, it is not the preferred material for tambour embroidery. But my advice is nevertheless: if you'd like to use the tambour hook, just try! Each tissue is different. Making swatches will make you see if the fabric works for you in your particular situation.

To get the stretch out of the fabric, you can "stabilize" it. For this purpose, you reinforce the jersey with a piece of embroidery film with is available from wholesalers or embroidery shops. Alternatively you can use a piece of silk organza. The embroidery will look good and you don't have to cope with the stretch of the fabric.

For stabilizing, place the fabric flat in front of you on the table with the wrong side up. Put a piece of foil or organza, without folds or creases, on top of it. Pin the layers together. Baste the fabric and the foil or organza together, not only to the sides but also around the embroideries, for added strength. These threads are getting pulled out after embroidering.

The characteristic of the tricot – the elasticity of the material – will not be compromised if you avoid stabilizing the whole piece of fabric. For that reason, remove as much as possible of the film or organza after you have finished the embroidery.

You can use embroidery in two different ways: scattered all over or isolated on specific parts. Scattered all over implicates the use of delicate silk organza for the whole garment. Is this a necessity? Not necessarily so. As I told earlier, the silk organza is beautiful, but fragile. If you use the silk organza for the whole garment, you'll probably line it with other material to cover the body and give the garment more structure. You can use other fabrics once you master the tambour hook. The fabric might not be see-through, but you can still feel the beads with your fingers and correct yourself by turning the frame around to see whether they are put in place.

MORE THAN JUST HAUTE COUTURE

So what are your options when you just start exploring this new technique? It depends on your background, your ambitions and your time.

Perfect examples of smaller projects to start with are:

- bracelets
    - applications for fashion or handmade bags or hats
    - covers for iPhone and iPad
    - book covers
    - cuffs
    - Collars

* * *

You may find some examples with patterns on a special page of my website: http://tinyurl.com/jf3lz9u.

You can make several smaller items on the fabric on your frame before you take it out. Taken seriously, these projects are small enough to enjoy making while learning along the way. By finishing smaller projects, you gather the needed experience to start bigger projects. And off you go!

You don't have to stick with your interpretations. You'll find beautiful forms all around you. Take them into your design and transform them into unique masterpieces. Your presentation can stand out with your choice of materials and techniques. Take a chance and just try. Make pictures and discuss ways to make your work better each time. Ask other people for feedback to help you look with different eyes. And step by step you will find your voice.

* * *

Working together with other people can propel your development. I used to share time sewing, discussing and sharing information with a dear friend for years on a regular basis. We both learned a lot and enjoyed our precious time together. You can find a companion as well. Many people search for another 'fanatic' in their field. There is so much beauty to be shared! A simple question might change your life.

Look for more inspiration here: http://tinyurl.com/juznnt5.

CHAPTER TEN
Epilog

ALMOST THERE

So you finished the book! Congratulations. I hope you enjoyed it. If you have any comments, please send an email to saskia@saskiaterwelle.nl

And with your first purchase at my Etsy Shop, I offer you a discount of 10,00 euro with the use of the following discount code: BOOKCOUPON46AWERWEO with your initial purchase of 100,00 euro or more.

If you are interested in taking courses in Broderie d'Art, please have a look at my website http://www.saskiaterwelle.com.

There are several ways to follow courses, from online courses with video materials and special Facebook groups, to courses in the atelier in the historical town of Doesburg, The Netherlands. This small city is a nice 'escape to the country' where you can enjoy both culture and nature. I will happily help you find appropriate accommodation if you want to stay a while.

The Atelier is a place for education and inspiration. We are an accredited work placement company where we train professionals. We are open to internships.

This book is part of the Haute Couture Embroidery Series, dedicated to creating and designing rich embroideries as in Parisian haute couture.

Other volumes will cover the following:

Finding inspiration
    Adding volume in different ways
    How to design a pattern
    How to prepare by making samples
    How to calculate materials
    Patterns for beginning embroiderers
    Patterns for advanced embroiderers

LET'S CONNECT

I would be honored to get in touch with you. Stay tuned and up-to-date with news about Broderie d'Art by signing up to my newsletter here: http://tinyurl.com/gstz6uk.

My website: http://www.saskiaterwelle.com

Printed in Poland
by Amazon Fulfillment
Poland Sp. z o.o., Wrocław

50600877R00037